O

love poems from the ozarks

d a v e   m a l o n e

ts T. S. Poetry Press • New York

T. S. Poetry Press
Ossining, New York
Tspoetry.com

ISBN 978-0-9898542-6-9
cover photo by l.l. barkat

Library of Congress Cataloging-in-Publication Data:
Malone, Dave
        [Poems.]
        O: love poems from the ozarks/Dave Malone
        ISBN 978-0-9898542-6-9

Library of Congress Control Number: 2015931626

for jenni

Contents

III. Autumn

IV. Winter

From the Poet

Teen Magazine. That awful glossy mag from the late 80s and early 90s. With covers and spreads of girl crush stars like Scott Baio and Leif Garret.

But there was also, *blue of the heaps of beads*.

The Diane Wakoski poem, "Blue Monday," once perched near the back of the magazine, perhaps between a shampoo ad and the latest poofy hairstyle.

In high school, my sister and I, only eighteen months apart in age, were good friends. I can't recall if my literature-inclined sister (teen mags notwithstanding) told me to read the poem, or if I thumbed the glossy pages of the edition seeking pics of bikini-clad girls, or if the roots of my lifelong passion to understand the intelligence, feelings, and power of women took over—but nonetheless. *Blue of the heaps of beads* grew in my head.

This was not an ordinary love poem.

There was a man in a blue suit. There was a fedora. Blood pooled on the street.

My sophomore year of college, I decided not to date. Instead, I wanted to understand women. I figured a purity and openness might occur without the dating and sexual element (as much as is possible with nineteen-year-olds). And I learned how to listen, and though the mysterious wants and desires of women still seemed distant, I felt I now knew something of compassion and of the heart.

By my junior year, my poetry-reading list grew to include powerful, memorable influences such as Fred Chappell's prose poem "Midquest," which featured the ebullience of his lover bathing.

The amazing, Midwestern, earthy, dark, mysterious poems of Jack Driscoll. I gulped Anne Sexton's love poems and Marge Piercy's and Sylvia Plath's, and of course, Diane Wakoski's.

I knew it necessary for a good writer to have life experiences, so at the age of twenty-two, I cashed my grandmother's college graduation gift check and drove my ugly but reliable Toyota Tercel across the south and east from Biloxi to Manhattan. At twenty-three, I moved in with two girls in Albuquerque. At twenty-six, armed with a graduate degree in English, I unsuccessfully tried to pull a Raymond Carver and worked as a janitor. At twenty-seven, I became a newspaper editor. I have worked in medical billing, at a semi-trailer factory, at a city parks and rec, and in academia. During those renegade times, I loved a couple of women, and I believe they loved me.

Blue of the heaps of beads.

When I was thirty, I prepared a full-length collection of my love poems which embody a passionate, romantic take on life set against both city and the Ozarks. I was brave enough to mail Diane Wakoski my manuscript with a request for a back-cover blurb. On a summer day in 1998, she responded by letter, writing magic about my volume: "Could it be that sex and love actually belong together? How nice to still embrace that rather literary idea." And I wept in the post office.

Since that time, I've published four more books of poetry. The landscape is similar. It is Ozark. It is woman in all her magnificence. It is passion and pain.

Blue of the heaps of beads.

I always come back to the love poem, and I always come back to the Ozarks.

Through interesting twists of fate that included a town barber, a drifter, and a snowstorm, I found Jenni here in southern Missouri. In ninth century Japan, it was customary for lovers via courier to exchange poems celebrating their romance. Many of the poems in this volume were ones I originally sent to Jenni. Often, I was the courier, delivering them in the shadowy, Ozark night. Other times, my biking messenger, James, (who looked a lot like this poet) brought them to her workplace. Sometimes, a poem rested on our bedside table, ready for us to read together at night.

Given the rich natural world where she and I live, given our roots, it was of course natural that southern Missouri, our hills and hollers, the lake, and our little burg between a pair of Ozark knobs would provide the backdrop for my love poems to her, for this work.

I wanted to capture passion but not stay away from the flawed nature of love. To love the shy backs of someone's knees, his or her unfairness—these encompass what we don't always discuss about our lovers. But I want to say what cannot be said. These revelations are my *blue of the heaps of beads*.

Dave Malone
Somewhere in the Ozarks
January 2015

I. Spring

We Blossom the World

What we can't say to each other blossoms the world.
Charges from our yard, the forsythia bushing out gold.

Runs into Ozark countryside as scent,
honeysuckle perfume intent on coupling.

The wetness of dew settling on beat-up barns,
the torn-up sky greening into tornado and your morning
    meanness.

The back forty sinkhole where I drop all my sins against you.
The poke greens and radishes daring to take out carrots you
    swore by.

The harps of daylight pouring through stained-glass of all the
    religious.
Church bells ringing out crisp as hearts.

Hips

Early morning, the earth is nothing.

The sprawling mocha wood sleeps,
the blond fescue still.

Then, the golden prairie flames,
the timber plain consumed.

Spring Dress

I love the unknown in you,
the unfair, the shy backs of your knees,
the colony of dimples
that sleep in moon-shaped huts

leaning

toward your mouth.

The Knobby Throat of Spring

Clouds shake with gray,
dancing a dirge of winter.
The house booms cold
like the solitary space
within a canon's bore.
A burst of sunlight chases
away grizzly April.
Beside the pond, a lark.
With her gullet charged,
a fillet of steel.

Romantic Theater

Spring days, the bruising redbuds
eclipse our town square of brick and awning.

Spring nights, the thicket of crickets
drowns our town in sugary chorus.

Yet, winged music nor purple bloom
usurps your theater—bedroom lights sizzle

beside a hushed set of onlooking eyes.

Tango

All the shadow selves
you and I clutch in the dark,
dance in the open doorway of loving—
bruises and safe words
inside the smack of tango.

Thunderboomer

April wind batters Ozark afternoon.
Redbuds bleed purple on the lawn.
Gray gnaws all the way down
to toe-stumbling roots.
Lightning forces squirrels into flight.
The house cries dark with hope
as you rise from the breakfast wasteland
we savored like hipbones.
I follow you into the bedroom
where you curl against me,
the gale smacking then cupping
the front door into giving up.
You are melty as butter.
Clouds blacken outside
like toast.

Hawksbill Crag

By gravel road
we rise four miles
into Ozark bluff.
Our truck hugs
the slant
of timber line
thin
as a pencil streak.

At Hawksbill Crag,
we tramp
thousands of feet
above shaggy pine
and the thumb of Jehovah.

I clutch a walking stick,
while you slide to the edge
of the bluff face
and act as if you
plunge
to
your
death
until you
slip off

the boulder
back into
the buttonholes
of the pines.

Lupercalia

Let the youth
be blooded
and wild.
Let them flee
the hilltop cave
and wreck our town
with tattered goat skins
and ripped laughter.
Let the girls
be whip-struck
by nude boys
until legs part
like bleeding orchid petals.
Let the older hearts
abandon the work
of tilling the soil
in fading winter sun—
for they, too,
once flooded the streets
with blood.

Ode to the Woman Fish on Norfork Lake

You dive
into the lake
where the GPS
charts a depth
of 82.3 feet,
but your arms
as fins
just dip
inside
the ruffled pillows
of waves
before I can
make my anguish
known to you.

I dread the deep
that is more
than bottom-feeding,
cigar-smoking,
whiskers-long-as-Pujols'-hitting-streaks
catfish—
but before
I can rope feeling
into language,
you rise from death,
a floating spear.

Landscape

Your body rolls
as deep and dark
as any Wyeth landscape—
and better.

The brown hills of Maine
toast
against limbs,
inlets of toes.

II. Summer

Photograph

The family pontoon attempts
to usurp dominant contrast
though your twin brother sticks out
his chest like a gangster—
your father's fedora
slopes too close to his nose.
Straight as the safety railing,
your older brother locks hands
on hips. He manages
a squint for the camera.

The boat blushes mimosa pink
to be upstaged by such a young girl
on a summer day meant for boating—
not the boasting of calves, thighs, shins,
white as cottonwood blossoms,
long as drooping pines spilling out
of timber trucks.

O those legs kill the middle,
crown themselves the dominant
and hold up the body
that's grown into the body I love—
the same quizzical eyes
which quicken me
when the camera shutter
blinks.

Longitude

Our bodies make the ocean from the bedroom
near abandoned town square, coyote, and hay baler.

The summer heat flexes trash-can muscle in our small-town
    ghetto.
Wind eats the curtains, spits beer on us in the four-post bed.

The moon a plum in the south your fingers find
when you rise up past the bush-league curve ball of my collar
    bone.

The clang of garbage-lid home plate beneath the tomgirl's slide
blooms your memory, so your fist curls into the craw of my knee.

The night turns traitor at our span and busts knuckles to break
    our longitude.
Darkness hustles through house and ceiling cracks to vault us into
    the lawn

where our legs rebel, stretch past South America,
now your mouth a river, my hair yucca—

until a morning frost when our vast frames reach far inside
the skinnydipping we insist on, a channel of arctic water.

Silk

The stretched wing of my tongue
floats above your belly until sweeping low
against your flower—the white trillium
that dresses the Amazon, cures snakebite,
this blossom of forest floor
I lip into ancient submission,
a wisp of rain in my mouth—
nature's silk holding only abandon.

You Can Deny

all day long
that your legs
aren't the apocalypse.
But I know
without heraldry
that hipbone
to ankle
defies gravity
and the devil
and announces
unto the world
the longitude
and latitude
of lands unseen—
of Coronado,
of hell on earth.

Fifth Innings

The starting pitcher tires
from wild pitches and crushed hopes to first.
The ump hitches his breast plate
searching for air while he dreams
of whiskey and steak.
Managers spit into the swirl of dusk light.
Fans drain dregs of beer,
shell even the tiniest peanuts
too lazy to clip the stairs
where vendors graze.
The box score yields nothing
of the fifth. Yet, the best of us
warm up as bull pen talent,
knowing the contest is only
half-way through,

Beyond Expectations

One comes to expect
the expected. But you break
the thumbs of expectations—
a bar bouncer twice your size
who folds in half
beneath the twist of your wrist.
You ring out in the whiskey night,
the roar of space
shuttling through atmosphere.
You snap all the galaxies
into pea pods of loving.
The pock-faced bouncer
can't return to work
because he doesn't know
what to do with broken thumbs
or sugar snap peas.

Hurt

What I said hurt you
then clipped me at the knees—
a Louisville Slugger in the meaty mitts
of Irish Joe who sold out to the Italian mafia
and banks his cash on horses and pain.
Because I can never take it back,
Joe summers in my head with flip flops
and girly martinis because he doesn't give a damn.

Conundrum of a Complex Man

In my darkest hours
when the stark moon glows
behind humid summer sweat,
do you wish me to be
clearer, hotter,
Venus claiming
the western sky?

Falafel King

You are the only one
for my simmering
chick peas,
diced onion,
fresh garlic
from the garden we planted
in stormy, Ozark weather.

I pour the flour
into a ceramic mixing bowl
and churn the spoils
until my fingers
crush the golden peas
into submission
then form the mixture
into tiny balls
worthy of grease.

I drop the bean batter
into flaming oil
as it sizzles
the second coming
of salvation—pop, pop!

New Life

One August, my grandmother wears blue jeans
and thumbs a ride from the Caney Mountain foothills
fifty miles north to the crest of Cedar Gap
and the snaking Frisco line.

On as much steam as her own,
the locomotive crawls into old Las Vegas,
where she baptizes her legs
in the El Rancho swimming pool
just long enough to be snatched up
by a flashy suit.

By sundown, she wears the new life
of a showgirl who never returns home.
Gambler's dotted die latches at temple and wrist.
The only black and white she's known before—
local newsprint yielding stories
of falling hog prices,
bumper crops of peaches.

Ramp

In minutes,
you learn
the dance
of the chop saw—
bend,
hold,
sway,
kiss—
you are as much
tango dancer
as carpenter
while you build the ramp
to scoot your father
between kitchen
and clinic.

Your shoulders,
Amish-strong,
gleam in the July heat
of the garage.
Beneath the brow
of power,
your father's and your own,
your blue eyes
focus a cloud storm
on the action
of the saw.

What We Are

You and I don't fear commitment,
we fear the days of Ozark August—
interminable heat, mosquitoes long as teats,
the hazy white boredom
before autumn.

Enlightenment

Tantric gurus talk about getting lost in sex
as if God is a place to get to—
nevermind this moment.

August

Inside your dark lily,
the stout reed dips,
the stretched stalk,
the mound of petals,
the final day of summer.

III. Autumn

Unmarked

No calendars mark
the first day of autumn—
not even ones posted on suburban
double-wide fridges. No calendars
mark the flutter of wings—
your bone-colored skirt
crying above Blue Spring. No calendars
mark the first day of your period—
the blood dripping into pyramids
on river rock. No calendars
mark the flutter of romance—
I shoulder a nest into your thighs
and craft our hair into a tent. No calendars
mark the flutter of union—
we sleep beneath the sexed redbuds
purpling like bruises.

Separation

The moon looms as boring as it can get—
half-way through its period without the rising pulse
of ovulation, just a fat, unruly slice of Swiss cheese.
Sporting holes as well in its vocal chords.
The gangly moon, if it had a voice,
would drop notes small and squeaky—
a jilted lover's alto eclipsed by Dino fame.

Relationship

Mount Everest can't mount the final incline,
rush up breathless at its word-stealing expanse.

The moon does not sport craters for eyes
to gaze upon its craggy leas fueling lovers and science.

The Atlantic Ocean, despite her rushing waves,
can never begin to wet her wetness.

Aquaphobia

We hold jobs worth holding,
but every Monday we skip work
for the longboat of our bed—
this vessel stocked with coffee,
eggs, couscous, beer.
A sea-farer's dream
pimped out with oak posts,
sleek masts, and guts so fierce
the tide retreats.

Loving

Our backs break in loving—
and then the rest of us.
Your cave nose, my lily ankle.
Our bed gets lost inside our bodies
like a small boat dinking around the Pacific.
Mattress and box springs shudder
into the size of a baby's wrist,
the once-safe haven of sleep
disappears
inside our mouths.

Portrait of Your Legs

Your long legs are stalks of wheat, sliver of moon,
the best yard a quarterback ever sneaked,

the far-flung, misty rings of Saturn,
the flowers Georgia O'Keefe never painted,

the T-square that eludes all draftsmen,
the collar about my neck during Sunday lovemaking.

In your absence, soybeans mount a revolution, tides evade the
    shore,
Favre considers coming out of retirement—again.

Saturn yearns to join demoted Pluto,
Georgia contemplates poetry and life in Manhattan,

architects squash their drafting artists into T-bones,
and your long legs (*in absentia*) are simply the bruises about my
    neck.

Civil War

From the grass green comforter
and disheveled white sheets,
you and I hold sentinel for weeks.
The battle of our loving is a landscape
of canon and chipped maps and civil war,
a river of blood and backups—
in the booming release
as gunpowder flames again.

The Deep

In the deep sea
most beings
invisible—
at home in frigid water
and pressurized life
not fit for human consumption.

In the deep sea
you and I
invisible—
at home in frigid water
where we publish papers
on the *Turritopsis nutricula,*
both uncertain
if what survives the deep
goes unnamed.

IV. Winter

Language

Two poets, we try to wrangle language
into feeling—as lost as fledgling cowboys

locked between two chipped gates
as they slide down onto barebacks

of impossible broncs bent on shocking
iron and man. Language bucks the same

in starts and end stops, promises no forgiveness
to two bards, dropped into knee-high mud,

arms and legs tangled as if one corpse,
quarters dull our eyes, and lips only a solid line

save the glimmer of your bicuspid
(or perhaps mine) in fading rodeo lights.

Forget It

You can forget the poems
where love is
a cathedral
sacred rite
rose
or even
the black boot
in the face.
Above me
underneath me
inside me
you reign
submit
melt
into the microscopic
grandness
of the cosmos—
the thumbholds
of your hips
the glower
in your mouth music
the red curse circling
your breasts
O
this is
the unsung

the broken cathedral
the rose
the coffin
the daffodil underfoot
O
this is the tiny everything
this is the poem.

Sham

This poem is a
sham
more than any
infomercial or
sermon,
for this attempt
to speak
of what we do
in cast-iron-skillet
sizzled-out
midnight
bedroom,
in the waking
knee passion
and the blaze
of your thighs
stoked
by my three-day scruff,
and the eyequake of
you—
oh to blather on all this
is so much
pure quackery
it can't be a
poem.

Admission Price for Doubting Who Can Love a Poet

Mathematicians flooded our home.

They displayed diagrams of sexy lines and arcs.

The cognoscenti marched in the street.

They lipped poems with circular, pedantic rhythms.

Scientists rushed you at the mailbox.

They planted beakers and equations on the front lawn.

The media claimed tomfoolery, skullduggery.

Everyone was bent on destroying you.

But when evening turned crimson and shadow,

and you mounted the porch, your slicing forms of line

beheaded many a media mogul.

Lovers Disappear Inside Devil's Backbone

Love, let's go ahead and take time out of the equation.
It's just a featureless t anyway—little more than x
and even more self-conscious.

Let's put you and me together in a room—
in a black room, and we'll be brown and areolaed
and landscapey and long and sinewy and humped.

Let's go ahead and take the world out of the equation.
It's just a small w on the cosmos line of infinity anyway.

Mirror

Last week,
you made
a Nobel Prize-winning
scientist
finger a revolver
and take ten paces
upon himself
to fire
into the expanse
of what we all could be.

Ghosts

At dusk
this town
takes on more
than the tones
of the black
of bats—our burg
booms dark inside
these Ozark knobs. Tiny
bursts of electric lights

pose, perfectly still

as if an expert daguerreotypist
freezes the entire landscape
in time—

But wait—a vital blur—
no, not all our village
slips into a copper sheet of sleep.

Local Gods

Wednesday evenings at work, we glue frames
and slice colored mats to house keepsakes—

trips to Mexico, Disneyland, the Indy 500,
senior pictures, personal paintings,

the last photograph of a clipped youth.

On archival paper, we hold together lives
in both the present and forever,

townsfolk blooming into immortal gods.

The Boatman

In bed, we watch *Vertigo*
and marvel at the plot.
Madeline slips
into another episode,
and you too slide
to the other side.
Though you nestle
into my shoulder,
your eyes solid as quarters,
the boatman lingers
below the Golden Gate
ready to take you
between this life
and the other.

Bruising Beauty

No photographer
needs to cast you
in the orange glow
of the magic hour
to prove my point.
But how I'd like to hire
the Slayton family
to waltz in with their lighting kit
of umbrellas and strobes
and have them suffer
from a piece of you.

Propulsion

The moment
of coming
you bite
into space
a floating astronaut
lost
unmapped
destitute
save the extraordinary
expanse of
deepest black—
your eyelids
locked
flesh moon rock
that will never
crack
break
open
again.

Small Strangeness

Every woman is you and not you.
But all merely girls

like the seedlings that start stars—
humble nebula beginnings

while you glow glimmer fire
supernova through the night

that ruins the sky
shuts down cities—

it is this end of the world
star fire that you are,

that is the brilliance,
that is the hum,

that is what quiets every woman
into the small strangeness when she walks.

New Moon

At midnight, there is little
left in us—not even the final curve
of the waning crescent
before it disappears
into God.

And here we are—
the sad shaking of lunar dust
before it falls off the bone cliff
of your hips. My hands lost
in the emptiness of space.

In the finality of midnight
we break against sleep
and total darkness
only by touching heat
not seen—your belly, my thigh
boil
into being
the cycle of stars,
the slicing sword of Orion,
a swath of breath that ignites
the darkest night
into the tiny blade
of the new moon.

Reunion

That open stretch of highway is my palm.
Burgeoning pines sprout as my fingertips—
the long shadows, days apart.

The moon sits low, a reclining chair.
Stars burst above, your arms and thoughts—
until dawn.

Tiny Machine

For lovers like us, time moves
backwards and forwards,
the tiniest machine in your palm
you take out on Sundays
and spin like gears of a hand watch.

Dappled sunlight on the oak post bed
turns into dark threads of rain.
Before we can eat brunch,
we are adrift in snow
outside my first apartment.

Before we can speak the language
of knowing each other, the shorthand
for gardening and taking out the glorious trash,
we are dropped on a railroad bed.
Under the blue moon, a locomotive
churns through the pine forest.
Blinded, we weep like newborns
until arms join in the utter, forest dark.

Acknowledgments

The author and publisher wish to express their grateful acknowledgment to the following publications and venues in which these poems and essays first appeared:

CircleShow: "Admission Price for Doubting Who Can Love a Poet" (as "They Learned the Hard Way")

Elder Mountain: A Journal of Ozark Studies: "How You Lasso the World," "Ode to the Woman Fish on Norfork Lake" (forthcoming), and "Photograph"

Every Day Poems: "Hips"

Flutter: "Portrait of Your Legs"

Gingko Tree Review: "We Blossom the World" (forthcoming)

The Meadow: "Unmarked" (as "No Calendars")

offcourse: "Beyond Expectations," "Lovers Disappear Inside Devil's Backbone," and "Mirror"

Rose and Thorn Journal: "Forget It"

San Pedro River Review: "Civil War" (as "The Far Side") and "Tiny Machine"

Storm Country Anthology (Missouri and Joplin Writers Guild): "Thunderboomer"

Thin Air: "You Can Deny"

Willows Wept Review: "New Moon"

"Fifth Innings," "Hawksbill Crag" and "Prairie Fire" originally appeared in *Seasons in Love* (Trask Road Press, 2012).

"Hawksbill Crag" also appeared in *Yonder Mountain: An Ozarks Anthology* (University of Arkansas Press, 2013).

"Landscape" was published online at *Wonder Book of Poetry*, a self-proclaimed "conversation in text, image and music."

"Lupercalia" first appeared on davemalone.net on February 14, 2014.

A portion of "Your Spring Dress" aired on NPR's *Tell Me More*, "Muses and Metaphors" on April 16, 2012.

Portions or earlier versions of "Loving," "Small Strangeness," and "Tango appeared in *Literary Sexts Anthology* (Words Dance Publishing, 2014).

Also from T. S. Poetry Press

Love, Etc.: Poems of Love, Laughter, Longing & Loss, by L.L. Barkat

Delicate, suggestive, clever.

—Carl Sharpe, editor at *VerseWrights*

How to Read a Poem: Based on the Billy Collins Poem "Introduction to Poetry", by Tania Runyan

No reader, experienced or new to reading poems, will want to miss this winsome and surprising way into the rich, wonderful conversations that poetry makes possible.

—David Wright, Assistant Professor of English at Monmouth College, IL

The Whipping Club, by Deborah Henry (an Oprah selection)

Multilayered themes of prejudice, corruption and redemption with an authentic voice and swift, seamless dialogue. A powerful saga of love and survival.

—*Kirkus Reviews* (starred review)

T. S. Poetry Press titles are available online in e-book and print editions. Print editions also available through Ingram.

tspoetry.com